DANIEL

SPIRITUAL LIVING IN A SECULAR WORLD

DOUGLAS CONNELLY

12 STUDIES FOR INDIVIDUALS OR GROUPS

T0339073

Life
Builder
Study

ivp

INTER-VARSITY PRESS
36 Causton Street, London SW1P 4ST, England
Email: ivp@ivpbooks.com
Website: www.ivpbooks.com

Originally published in the United States of America in the LifeGuide® Bible Studies series in 1986 by InterVarsity Press, Downers Grove, Illinois
Second edition published 2000
First published in Great Britain by Scripture Union in 2000
This edition published in Great Britain by Inter-Varsity Press 2018

British Library Cataloguing-in-Publication Data
A catalogue record for this book is available from the British Library.

ISBN: 978–1–78359–800–7

Printed in Great Britain by Ashford Colour Ltd, Gosport, Hampshire

Inter-Varsity Press publishes Christian books that are true to the Bible and that communicate the gospel, develop discipleship and strengthen the church for its mission in the world.

IVP originated within the Inter-Varsity Fellowship, now the Universities and Colleges Christian Fellowship, a student movement connecting Christian Unions in universities and colleges throughout Great Britain, and a member movement of the International Fellowship of Evangelical Students. Website: www.uccf.org.uk. That historic association is maintained, and all senior IVP staff and committee members subscribe to the UCCF Basis of Faith.

Contents

Getting the Most
Out of *Daniel*

In the sweep of great world empires, what happens to a few people is usually overlooked. When the city of Jerusalem fell into the hands of the mighty Babylonian army, it probably didn't make much of a stir in the ancient world. It was an event so insignificant to the Babylonians that they didn't even mention it in their official chronicles.

The conquest of Jerusalem in 605 B.C. was just the first of three defeats the people of Judah would suffer under the king of Babylon, Nebuchadnezzar. This time he simply established Babylonian authority over Judah and left. On the surface not much had changed. But behind the scenes a few Jewish families and some young Jewish men were changed forever. Nebuchadnezzar took a handful of young men from their homeland to Babylon and thrust them into a new lifestyle. Every effort was made to break down their convictions. They had to make a difficult choice. Would they hold to their faith and to a life of obedience to God, or would they flow into the new culture? It was a time of crisis for these young men, including the man we will be studying—Daniel.

It is precisely at this point that the experience of Daniel reaches out and grabs us. Regardless of how sheltered our childhood was or how often we were taken to church, there comes a time when we are thrust into an unbelieving world. We are confronted in the university or on the job or in social situations with a lifestyle radically different from what is taught in the Bible. At each turn we have difficult decisions to make. Will we obey God regardless of the consequences, or will we become part of the surrounding culture?

Daniel gives us practical and personal help in our struggle. He was a man who rose to a position of great influence and prestige in the world system but who never compromised essential biblical principles. He shows us how to live a life of spiritual integrity in the crush of a secular world. Anyone who has been tempted to cave in to the world's pressures can learn a lot from him.

Historical Framework

Israel's great king Solomon died in 931 B.C. Solomon's son Rehoboam foolishly provoked the leaders of the northern part of the nation, and they split off from the south. That disastrous division was never healed. The ten northern clans or tribes were now called Israel. The two southern clans were called Judah. Israel existed until 722 B.C., when it was destroyed by the Assyrians. Judah was spared until 586 B.C., when the Babylonian armies crushed the nation.

Nebuchadnezzar, the Babylonian commander, came to Judah and Jerusalem three times to put down Jewish rebellion against the authority of the empire. In 605 B.C. the Jews were treated fairly well. A few young men (including Daniel) were taken hostage, but the nation was left relatively undisturbed. The second time Nebuchadnezzar came (597 B.C.) the treatment was harsher. More people were deported to Babylon, including King Jehoiachin and the prophet Ezekiel. Finally, in 586 B.C. Babylonian patience was exhausted. The temple of God was burned, the walls of Jerusalem were broken down, and the people were either killed or deported to Babylon. A summary of these three conquests can be found in 2 Kings 24—25 and 2 Chronicles 36.

God judged Judah for seventy years (605-536 B.C.)—a period called the Babylonian captivity. In 536 B.C. Babylon was defeated by a new world power (Persia) and Cyrus (the Persian ruler) allowed the Jews to return to Judah.

Daniel's ministry in Babylon extended through the entire seventy-year captivity and into the reign of the Persians. Daniel lived well into his eighties or nineties! His primary focus as a prophet was on the Gentile (non-Israelite) nations. Even during the period of Judah's humiliation God's voice was heard in the courtroom of the emperor.

Theological Focus

If you read the book of Daniel and only see a den of lions and strange visions, you have missed the main character in the book—the sovereign God! Daniel wrote this book not to glorify himself but to exalt the Lord. In every circumstance, in every crisis, Daniel points us to a God who is at work in human history.

To say that God is sovereign simply means that nothing happens that is not planned or permitted by God. That is true of kingdoms and it is true of our lives. Daniel's God is not a weak, frustrated deity who sits in heaven, wringing his hands, hoping everything will turn out right. He is a God who orders all events according to his own will.

The book of Daniel is written in a literary form known as apocalyptic literature. Apocalyptic books speak to us in those times when God seems to be absent. The crushed people of Judah in Daniel's day were saying, "Where is God?" Daniel answers their questions by showing them that even in a national catastrophe God is working out his purpose and plan.

Daniel is able to resist compromise because of his relationship to the sovereign God. His obedience was simply an expression of God's kingship in his life. Daniel's courage to proclaim God's message came from his allegiance to the sovereign Lord who reigned as King, even above the kings of Babylon. Be prepared in this study to see God in a new way! It will be a stretching, convicting but life-changing adventure.

Daniel and the Future

The second part of the book of Daniel is less well-known and a lot more difficult to understand than the first part. But it is no less profitable! In Daniel 1—6 the focus is primarily on the life and character of Daniel as the *servant* of God. In Daniel 7—12 the focus is on Daniel as the *spokesperson* for God. These chapters consist of a series of visions given to Daniel—visions of the future of the Gentile nations (chapter 7) and of the surviving nation of Judah (chapters 8—12).

The visions of Daniel are a source of controversy among students of the Bible. The first area of controversy centers around the integrity of the visions. Scholars who are critical of the Bible maintain that what is recorded in these chapters is not prophecy at all. Instead these scholars claim that the author wrote these words *after* the events took place (some time in the second century B.C.). According to this view, these chapters record history (a catalog of events that have already transpired) and not prophecy (a prediction of events in the future).

For those who accept the Bible as God's truth, this controversy is settled by the claims of the book itself and by the defense of those claims by believing scholars. We also have Jesus' own confirmation of Daniel's existence. In Matthew 24:15 Jesus referred to Daniel as a real person and called him a "prophet." Jesus also quoted from these later chapters of Daniel and took them as authoritative revelation of truth from God (see Matthew 24:30; Luke 21:27).

The second area of controversy centers on the interpretation of the final six chapters of Daniel. Even Christians who agree on the historical integrity of Daniel disagree on how these visions should be interpreted. The objective in this guide is not to defend one particular prophetic system but rather to try to understand what Daniel says. The emphasis of each study is on what we can learn from this book about God's program for human history. Not all the answers about the future will be found in one part of God's Word. If we understand this part, however, we will have a better framework for understanding the rest of God's truth. We will gain far more from Daniel if we try to learn what is revealed here rather than defending a preconceived idea of what we want Daniel to say.

While Daniel 7—12 is not an easy-to-understand section of Scripture, it is just as much the Word of God as Daniel 1—6 or the Gospel of John or Romans, and as a result, it is beneficial for our growth in knowledge and obedience to God. After spending many hours in this book, I can assure you that this study will not only expand your understanding of God's program for the future of the world, but it will also expand your capacity to trust a sovereign God for your future. His eternal plan includes you!

Suggestions for Individual Study

1. As you begin each study, pray that God will speak to you through his Word.

2. Read the introduction to the study and respond to the personal reflection question or exercise. This is designed to help you focus on God and on the theme of the study.

3. Each study deals with a particular passage—so that you can delve into the author's meaning in that context. Read and reread the passage to be studied. If you are studying a book, it will be helpful to read through the entire book prior to the first study. The questions are written using the language of the New International Version, so you may wish to use that version of the Bible. The New Revised Standard Version is also recommended.

4. This is an inductive Bible study, designed to help you discover for yourself what Scripture is saying. The study includes three types of questions. *Observation* questions ask about the basic facts: who, what, when, where and how. *Interpretation* questions delve into the meaning of the passage. *Application* questions help you discover the implications of the text for growing in Christ. These three keys unlock the treasures of Scripture.

Write your answers to the questions in the spaces provided or in a personal journal. Writing can bring clarity and deeper understanding of yourself and of God's Word.

5. It might be good to have a Bible dictionary handy. Use it to look up any unfamiliar words, names or places.

6. Use the prayer suggestion to guide you in thanking God for what you have learned and to pray about the applications that have come to mind.

7. You may want to go on to the suggestion under "Now or Later," or you may want to use that idea for your next study.

Suggestions for Members of a Group Study

1. Come to the study prepared. Follow the suggestions for individual study mentioned above. You will find that careful preparation will greatly enrich your time spent in group discussion.

2. Be willing to participate in the discussion. The leader of your group will not be lecturing. Instead, he or she will be encouraging the members of the group to discuss what they have learned. The leader will be asking the questions that are found in this guide.

3. Stick to the topic being discussed. Your answers should be based on the verses which are the focus of the discussion and not on outside authorities such as commentaries or speakers. These studies focus on a particular passage of Scripture. Only rarely should you refer to other portions of the Bible. This allows for everyone to participate in in-depth study on equal ground.

4. Be sensitive to the other members of the group. Listen attentively when they describe what they have learned. You may be surprised by their insights! Each question assumes a variety of answers. Many questions do not have "right" answers, particularly questions that aim at meaning or application. Instead the questions push us to explore the passage more thoroughly.

When possible, link what you say to the comments of others. Also, be affirming whenever you can. This will encourage some of the more hesitant members of the group to participate.

5. Be careful not to dominate the discussion. We are sometimes so eager to express our thoughts that we leave too little opportunity for others to respond. By all means participate! But allow others to also.

6. Expect God to teach you through the passage being discussed and through the other members of the group. Pray that you will have an enjoyable and profitable time together, but also that as a result of the study you will find ways that you can take action individually and/or as a group.

7. Remember that anything said in the group is considered confidential and should not be discussed outside the group unless specific permission is given to do so.

8. If you are the group leader, you will find additional suggestions at the back of the guide.

1

Have You Got What It Takes?

Daniel 1

Several years ago our daughter decided that a semester of college away from home would be fun. We loaded all her stuff in a borrowed van and made the six-hour trip to her new home. After we hauled everything to her dorm room I kissed her goodbye and headed back. Tears streamed down my face as I left the campus. I was proud of Kim as she stepped into adulthood, but my joy was edged with the pain of letting her go.

GROUP DISCUSSION. Describe your own transition into adult responsibility or a time when you had to let go of someone you loved. What was the most difficult part of the process?

PERSONAL REFLECTION. Think back to when you first were on your own. What new adjustments did you have to make?

Daniel was torn from his home and family when he was only twelve or thirteen years old. He and a few other young men were taken eight hundred miles away to Babylon. They were enrolled in an intensive three-year training program designed to transform them into loyal Babylonian bureaucrats. A crisis of conscience erupted when the first meal was served. *Read Daniel 1.*

1. Trace Daniel's emotions through this chapter. How would Daniel feel in verse 3? in verse 8? in verse 15? in verse 20?

_____

2. What specific tactics were used to give Daniel and his friends a new Babylonian orientation (vv. 3-7)?

_____

3. How do these tactics parallel the pressures Christians face today in a secular society?

_____

4. Why were the food regulations of the Old Testament law so important to Daniel (vv. 8-10)?

Do you think he was making a big issue out of a minor problem? Explain.

_____

5. How can Christians today determine which activities we will engage in and which we won't?

_____

6. What steps did Daniel take to provide a creative alternative to the king's plan (vv. 11-14)?

7. What can you learn from Daniel's attitude and actions about how to respond when your biblical values are challenged?

---

8. What combination of factors produced the exceptional ability of Daniel and his friends (vv. 17-20)?

---

9. What aspect of Daniel's character or conduct in this chapter impresses you the most?

How can you cultivate that same quality in your own life?

Ask God to give you courage and wisdom to obey him when you feel pressured to compromise.

Now or Later

Other people in the Bible also took a stand for what was right when they were pressured to take the easy way out. If you need strength in that area of your life, you may want to study their examples.

Joseph: Genesis 39—41
David: 1 Samuel 17
Esther: Esther 4
Peter and John: Acts 4:13-31

2

A Disturbing Dream

Daniel 2:1-30

Scientists tell us that we dream every night—and most of the time we enjoy it. But some dreams terrorize us. They are the dreams C. S. Lewis called "dreams that make you afraid to sleep again."

GROUP DISCUSSION. Describe a memorable or recurring dream. Bring an object or article of clothing that illustrates some aspect of the dream. Tell or act out the dream with the same emotion you felt when you had the dream.

PERSONAL REFLECTION. Have you ever had a dream that was so real it almost seemed to be true? How did you feel when you woke up?

Powerful kings in ancient Babylon had dreams too! Mighty King Nebuchadnezzar had a dream that he couldn't forget. He knew it came from someone far greater than himself. *Read Daniel 2:1-30.*

1. What is your impression of Nebuchadnezzar as you look through the passage again? (What kind of man was he?)

2. Why do you think Nebuchadnezzar demanded to know the content of his dream from his wise men as well as the dream's interpretation (vv. 1-13)?

3. Imagine yourself in Daniel's situation. How would you and your closest friends respond, knowing that you faced certain death if you couldn't interpret a dream you knew nothing about?

4. From Daniel's example what can we learn about how we should react to a personal crisis (vv. 14-18)?

5. Compare how you normally respond when God answers your prayers with how Daniel responded in verses 19-23.

6. Verses 20-23 have been called "Daniel's psalm" because of their exaltation of God. What aspects of God's character are emphasized in these verses?

7. How will knowledge of God's wisdom authority and power change how you view your next crisis?

8. What did Daniel want King Nebuchadnezzar to know about the true God (vv. 27-30)?

_____

9. Three aspects of Daniel's spiritual maturity stand out in this chapter: his *wisdom* in response to a crisis, his *prayer* in response to a problem and his *praise* in response to God's work in his life. Which of those marks of maturity is most well-developed in your life?

which of them is weakest?

_____

10. Based on Daniel's example, what specific steps will you take to strengthen your weak area?

Ask God to remind you of his character and his promises when you face a personal crisis.

Now or Later

Using Daniel's psalm as a model (2:20-23), compose your own psalm or expression of praise to God. Thank him for aspects of his character that have been displayed through his work in your life. Pray or sing the psalm back to God as an expression of adoration. Share the psalm with someone else as a testimony of your trust in the Lord.

3

Facing
the Future

Every year tabloid headlines in the grocery store checkout lanes shout the same promises—bold predictions for the new year from the world's most notable psychics and fortunetellers! Some of the predictions are obvious, some are moronic, most never happen. But every year thousands of people buy copies hoping for some glimpse into the future.

GROUP DISCUSSION. Make a prediction about the next twelve months of your life. How confident are you that the prediction will come true?

PERSONAL REFLECTION. What would you most like to know about your own future? Who would you trust to give you a reliable prediction?

Daniel 2 is one of the most amazing predictive chapters in the Bible. It was written around 600 B.C., yet it accurately described the future rise and fall of four great empires! Some of Daniel 2 may seem like so much ancient history to us, but it was all future to Daniel. He peered through future centuries with God's eyes. *Read Daniel 2:31-49.*

---

1. From your study in Daniel so far, summarize the events that led to Daniel's appearance before King Nebuchadnezzar.

2. Nebuchadnezzar had demanded that any interpreter of his dream had to first tell him what happened in the dream. What about Daniel's description of the dream (vv. 31-35), would have caused Nebuchadnezzar to be troubled (2:1)?

3. In the interpretation of the king's dream, why do you think God referred to Nebuchadnezzar as the head of gold (vv. 36-38)?

4. What observations can you make about the relative value and comparative strength of the four metals making up the statue (vv. 31-33)?

5. While Daniel does not identify the future kingdoms, we know them as the Medo-Persian (silver), the Greek (bronze) and the Roman (iron) empires. What does your answer to question 4 and what Daniel says in verses 36-43 tell you about the nature, organization and strength of these kingdoms?

6. What can you conclude about the kingdoms represented by the mixture of clay (ceramic) with iron (vv. 41-43)?

7. Verse 44 says that "in the time of those kings [the ones represented by the toes of the statue], the God of heaven will set up a kingdom." How would you describe the kingdom of God based on verses 44-45?

8. In your opinion, was this prophecy fulfilled when Jesus established the church or is it referring to the still future kingdom? Explain.

---

9. Describe the king's response to Daniel's interpretation of his dream (vv. 46-49).

---

10. What does this chapter teach you about God's activity in the unfolding of human history?

---

11. How does the portrait of God in this chapter encourage you to trust him with your life and circumstances?

Take time to thank God for his control over the present and the future.

Now or Later

Almost 1,200 years before Daniel, God gave another powerful ruler a dream about the future, and another young man interpreted the dream when the pagan magicians had failed. Joseph interpreted the Pharaoh's dream and saved God's people from starvation. You can read the story in Genesis 41. Consider: Does God still speak to us in dreams? What authority can we use to determine if a dream is genuinely from God?

4

Bow or Burn!

Daniel 3

Most of us have never had to face death or persecution for our commitment to Jesus Christ—but that doesn't mean the pressure is off! The secular culture in which we live has other ways of pushing us away from wholehearted obedience to the Lord. If you've ever revealed your faith convictions in a university classroom or turned down an invitation to the wrong kind of entertainment on a business trip, you have felt the pressure to compromise in order to be accepted by others.

GROUP DISCUSSION. In what circumstances have you been pressured to compromise what is right?

What resources can help you resist that pressure?

PERSONAL REFLECTION. Think of someone who is a model to you of courageous commitment to Christ. How can you learn more from that person about remaining faithful in your allegiance to Christ?

The story of Shadrach, Meshach and Abednego in the fiery furnace ranks among the top ten best-known Bible stories. It's so familiar that sometimes we forget it really happened! It's also a very instructive account for men and women who are trying to live for God in a secular society. *Read Daniel 3.*

1. If you were covering this story for the evening news, what scenes would you include in the final edit?

Which participants would you try to interview and why?

2. What do you think prompted Nebuchadnezzar to build this image of gold (vv. 1-7)?

3. What motivated the astrologers to report the disobedience of Shadrach, Meshach and Abednego (vv. 8-12)?

4. What temptations did Shadrach, Meshach and Abednego face when they were brought before the king (vv. 13-15)?

5. What were these men certain of in their response to Nebuchadnezzar's challenge, and what were they uncertain of (vv. 16-18)?

6. How will their example encourage you if you are faced with the possibility of losing your job or being rejected by friends because of your refusal to compromise God's Word?

7. Some Christians claim that pain or sickness or difficulty are always the result of sin or lack of faith. How would you respond to that claim in light of verses 16-18?

8. What specific actions did God take to assure the three men and to demonstrate his power to Nebuchadnezzar (vv. 24-30)?

9. As you look back over the chapter, what lessons about the risks and rewards of obedience to God are most significant to you?

10. What commitments can you make to the Lord today that will prepare you to face the pressures of the secular culture around you?

Renew your commitment to Jesus as Lord over your life. Ask him to give you the courage and grace to seek to please him first of all.

Now or Later

Reading the accounts of Christians who have been persecuted or martyred for their faith will give you a deeper appreciation for those who are suffering for their allegiance to Christ. Two books that will challenge you are *By Their Blood: Christian Martyrs in the Twentieth Century* by James and Marti Hefley (Baker, 1996), and *Martyrs*, edited by Susan Bergman (HarperSanFrancisco, 1996). A search of Christian periodicals or Web sites will show you where Christians are being persecuted today. Spend some time praying for Christians who are under persecution.

5

Our God Reigns!

Daniel 4

The man sitting across from me in the restaurant had lost everything. First his high-profile, lucrative position in the automotive world was slashed in a corporate restructuring plan. In the emotional and economic shakeup that followed, his wife divorced him and his children withdrew in angry silence. He parked cars to make ends meet. When everything else was gone, the Lord was waiting. In the bleakest days of his existence, my friend found genuine life and happiness by trusting in the one person who would never abandon him. He is determined, with God's help, to restore his family relationships. God brought him to the end of his rope in order to rescue him forever.

GROUP DISCUSSION. Describe your most humbling experience. What positive change came from that ordeal?

PERSONAL REFLECTION. Do you rely most on the Lord in times of prosperity or in times of difficulty? Why?

We are not accustomed to hearing national leaders name their sins in public. That's why Daniel 4 is such an unusual chapter! Nebuchadnezzar, the great, proud, powerful king, writes a letter to the world describing how God humiliated him for seven years and then graciously restored him. *Read Daniel 4.*

1. How does Nebuchadnezzar's proclamation in 4:1-3 differ from what he said about God in 3:28-29 (after the fiery furnace)?

2. As you read Nebuchadnezzar's description of the dream (vv. 9-18), what aspects of it might have caused the king to be "terrified" (v. 5)?

3. God's purpose for giving the dream is repeated three times (vv. 17, 25, 32). Why do you think God was so intent on impressing Nebuchadnezzar with his absolute authority instead of his grace or love?

4. If verse 17 is applicable today, must we conclude that Adolf Hitler, Joseph Stalin and other evil rulers came to power by God's decree? Explain.

How does your response relate to (or challenge) your perception of who God is and how he acts?

5. If Nebuchadnezzar had repented of his sins as Daniel advised, do you think God would have withheld his judgment, or was his decision irrevocable at this point (vv. 24-27)? Explain.

6. Why did God wait a full year between the announcement of judgment and its actual fulfillment (v. 29)?

---

7. What specific steps did God take to humble Nebuchadnezzar (vv. 31-33)?

---

8. A new Nebuchadnezzar came out of this experience. He gives God glory instead of himself (vv. 34-37). Do you think he was simply forced into humility by God, or was there a genuine change of attitude? Explain.

---

9. Sometimes we gain fresh insight into God's character as we wrestle with the truth. What's the hardest thing about this chapter for you to accept?

What does that hard lesson teach you about how God works in our lives to bring us to spiritual maturity and Christlikeness?

Express to God your trust in his control over the world and his care over your life.

Now or Later

Is there a "stump" in your life—the reminder of a "tree" of your own efforts that was cut down? What is God trying to teach you through that painful experience? Did you learn the lesson or are you still resisting God?

6

The Handwriting on the Wall

Daniel 5

God doesn't often use committees or large groups to do his greatest works. Most often God finds just one person who is totally committed to him, and then God works powerfully though that person to accomplish what he desires. When God's people seem weak and ineffective, the problem is never God's ability but the availability of one woman or one man through whom he will demonstrate his power. Never underestimate the influence of one godly life.

GROUP DISCUSSION. What one person has had the most influence on you? Has that influence been positive or negative?

PERSONAL REFLECTION. How do you want to be remembered by the people who are closest to you?

What are you doing each day to cultivate the influence you want to leave behind?

As chapter five opens, Daniel is more than eighty years old. The successors to Nebuchadnezzar's throne have ignored him. He has been shuffled off to some obscure office in the Babylonian bureaucracy. But when the king finds himself in trouble, he calls on God's man. Daniel shows us how to stand for God over the long haul. *Read Daniel 5.*

1. If this chapter were being produced as a motion picture, what musical background would be playing in verse 1? verse 5? verse 18? verse 30?

2. The events in this chapter take place in 539 B.C., the year (the very night) of the fall of Babylon to the Medo-Persian army led by Cyrus the Great. The Babylonians considered their city impregnable. They had twenty years of food supplies on hand and the fresh water of the Euphrates River flowed through the heart of the city. With that background, what do you think motivated Belshazzar to have this feast?

3. How would you have reacted if you had been at the banquet and saw a hand appear and write on the wall (v. 5)?

4. Three times Daniel recorded the failure of the "wise men" of Babylon to interpret the message of God. What point is Daniel trying to make?

5. What insights into the nature of Belshazzar's sins can you find in verses 18-23?

6. When are you tempted toward similar sins?

7. How can Daniel's words to Belshazzar help us become more humble and thankful to God (vv. 18-24)?

8. Why do you think Daniel emphasizes that "that very night" the city of Babylon fell and Belshazzar was killed (v. 30)?

9. How does this chapter demonstrate that seventy years of life under Babylon's influence had not broken down Daniel's convictions?

10. What can we learn from Daniel's example that will help us resist pressures to compromise our convictions?

Ask God to give you a positive, God-honoring influence on people around you.

Now or Later

Think of some present-day examples of people who mock God by their words or actions. Does God seem slow to judge their mockery? How can you explain God's "slowness"?

7

On the Menu at the Lions' Club

Daniel 6

Your first day on the job you meet the enemy and don't even know it. Later, the company gives you a promotion, a raise and a new office—all the things you deserve for your hard work and creative ideas. The only problem is that a few of your coworkers aren't too happy it. They determine to bring you down any way they can.

GROUP DISCUSSION. Tell the group about a time when you were betrayed or accused unjustly of doing wrong. What do you think motivated the person who attacked you?

PERSONAL REFLECTION. What would you have to "clean out" before your boss or spouse looked through your desk, locker or favorite Internet sites?

Daniel in the lions' den is a story we never get tired of hearing. I've always been impressed by this story because Daniel was not thrown into the lions' den for being bad, but for being godly! We expect to be punished when we do wrong, and when we do right we expect to be promoted. That is certainly the ideal, but it doesn't always work out that way. Sometimes those who do wrong are rewarded and those who do right are persecuted. *Read Daniel 6.*

1. List three or four words that describe each of the main characters in this account. How would you describe them to your best friend?

_____

2. What can we conclude about Daniel's character from the results of this special investigation by his enemies (vv. 4-5)?

_____

3. If you were being watched as Daniel was, what changes (if any) would you want to make in your present lifestyle?

_____

4. King Darius willingly signed the document prohibiting prayer (vv. 6-9). How does this action resemble the sins of his predecessors?

_____

5. Daniel had three choices in response to the king's decree: (1) stop praying for thirty days, (2) pray secretly or (3) pray as usual. Explain the consequences of each and why you think Daniel made the choice he did.

Which choice would you have made?

_____

6. How do verses 14-20 underscore the impact Daniel's life had on the king?

7. In what ways would the miracle Darius witnessed have reinforced Daniel's personal example (vv. 21-24)?

8. What specific aspects of God's character can you discover in Darius's decree praising the "God of Daniel" (vv. 25-27)?

9. How has Daniel encouraged you to be a more Christlike example to those around you?

10. What can you learn from Daniel's experience that will help you trust God even in the face of the threat of punishment for your obedience to God?

Ask God to show you areas where your personal integrity needs to be strengthened. Follow up with an obedient response.

Now or Later

The events in Daniel 6 happened when Daniel was more than eighty years old. Compare Daniel's actions in this chapter with his actions in chapter one when he was only fifteen years old. Reflect on what it took for Daniel to live such a consistent life of obedience to God for more than seventy years in the corrupt society of Babylon.

8

A Prophetic Panorama

Daniel 7

Have you ever wondered where human history is going—or how it will end? Nations and empires rise, expand, weaken and fall. Leaders live, rule and die. But where is everything headed? Some people say that history is going nowhere. Others try to sound more optimistic and say that history is going wherever humans take it. Christians who know God's Word, however, realize that history has a plan. God is not sitting in heaven hoping everything will work out. He has already told us how history will conclude because he has planned it all.

GROUP DISCUSSION. What are some ways that people think the world will come to an end?

PERSONAL REFLECTION. What one question would you like to ask God about the future?

Why do you want to know the answer?

God gave Daniel several visions of the future. This one began as a terrifying dream. *Read Daniel 7.*

---

1. What scene from Daniel's vision would you most like to have recorded on videotape?

2. If you had seen this vision with Daniel, what question would you have asked the one who interpreted the vision for Daniel?

3. The sea is used in many prophecies to represent the nations of the world. If that is the picture here, how would you explain verses 2-3?

4. Daniel sees four beasts which, according to verse 17, represent four kingdoms. The lionlike appearance of the first beast may represent that kingdom's strength and majesty. What characteristics of the second, third and fourth kingdoms are suggested by verses 5-7?

5. What aspects of God's nature and power are suggested by Daniel's description of the Ancient of Days in verses 9-10?

6. How can this vision of God give us hope and stability when the nations (or our lives) are in turmoil?

7. The final figure to appear in Daniel's vision is "one like a son of man" (vv. 13-14), an apparent description of Jesus. What effect does his coming have on the inhabitants and rulers of the world?

8. After the four kingdoms rise, "the saints of the Most High will receive the kingdom" (vv. 17-18). How is their conquest different from that of the four kingdoms?

9. Describe the political and military power of the "other horn" from the information found in this chapter (vv. 19-26).

10. What can you conclude about the moral and spiritual character of the "other horn"?

11. Twice the heavenly interpreter says that the last king will be tried and condemned by God (vv. 22, 26). Why do you think God goes to the effort of setting up court to judge someone so blatantly sinful?

12. Daniel is told that the saints of the Most High will share in the kingdom with the "one who is like a son of man." What do you find most appealing about Daniel's description of God's kingdom (vv. 13-14, 27) and why?

Ask God to give you confidence in his power and plan for the future.

Now or Later

Can you think of any animals that represent modern super-power nations? What "beastly" character traits would God assign to these nations?

9

Superpowers in Conflict

During some difficult days in my own life, I prayed often that God would give me a glimpse of my future. Would I be able to support my family? Would I ever regain the respect and trust I had lost? Would I even survive? I never received those glimpses—and in God's time the difficult days ended. But at times I still find myself wishing I could just get a peek at what's ahead.

GROUP DISCUSSION. If God offered to show you snapshots of your nation's future over the next two hundred years, would you want to see them? Why or why not?

PERSONAL REFLECTION. What would you like to know about the next ten years of your life? Do you think that knowledge would make you happier or more secure?

Daniel's vision of the future gets very personal beginning in chapter eight. The first seven chapters stress the destinies of the Gentile (non-Jewish) world powers. In chapters 8-12 the emphasis is on the destiny of Israel, Daniel's own people. *Read Daniel 8.*

---

1. As you look through the chapter again, pick out the main images in

Daniel's vision (vv. 1-14) and then list the matching interpretation of each image in verses 15-27.

---

2. The two-horned ram that Daniel sees represents the kings of the Medo-Persian empire. From the events portrayed in verses 3 and 4, how would you expect this kingdom to come on the world scene?

---

3. The goat with one horn is a symbol of the Greek empire and their notable king Alexander the Great (v. 21). From the scene in verses 5-8, how would you describe the clash of the Greek empire (the goat) with the Persian empire (the ram)?

---

4. Based on the knowledge and experience you have gained thus far in the "interpretation of visions" with Daniel as a guide, how would you interpret the symbolism of verses 9-12?

---

5. The "stern-faced king" (v. 23) Gabriel describes is probably Antiochus Epiphanes, a Greek-speaking king who ruled Syria and Palestine from 175 to 164 B.C. He hated the Jews and their God. His most infamous act was desecrating the temple in Jerusalem in 168 B.C. For more than six years ("2,300 evenings and mornings," v. 14) Antiochus oppressed the people of Israel. Finally, the Jews were able to drive Antiochus out of Israel and to reclaim the temple. If you had been a Jew living under the tyranny of Antiochus, how would it have made you feel to read Daniel's prophetic prediction of the very events you were experiencing?

6. What specific qualities can you see in Antiochus that you might also expect to see in an evil ruler bent on world conquest?

7. In what ways would this chapter be an encouragement to Christians living under political tyranny (or even emotional discouragement or spiritual attack)?

8. How does this chapter fit with Daniel's main theme of God's absolute authority?

9. What perspective does this chapter give us in understanding how a good God can permit evil?

Pray for Christians who are being persecuted for their faith. Ask God to give them assurance of his absolute authority even over evil oppressors.

Now or Later

Daniel's predictions were fulfilled precisely and literally. Should we expect biblical predictions about our future to be fulfilled in the same way? Explain.

10

Kneeling on God's Promises

Daniel 9

Sometimes reading just one passage of the Bible will change the way we pray. One day I confided in an older, more mature believer that my prayers for the sick seemed ineffective. "I've never seen God raise up someone from sickness powerfully, miraculously," I said. "I know he is able to heal, but so far he hasn't done it."

My friend's response was simple, but it pierced to the heart of the problem. "Have you ever asked God to heal someone miraculously?"

I began to defend my prayers, but all that came out was "no."

"James 4:2 says that you do not have because you do not ask God," he said.

From that day on I began to pray differently.

GROUP DISCUSSION. Tell the group about a time when you felt compelled to pray more intently than usual. What circumstances prompted you to seek God so earnestly?

PERSONAL REFLECTION. Based on the content of your prayers alone, what has concerned you most this past week?

One morning, shortly after the Babylonians had been conquered by the Medes and Persians, Daniel was reading the prophet Jeremiah. As

Daniel read Jeremiah's words, a couple of passages seemed to leap off the page (Jeremiah 25:8-12; 29:10-11). God promised that after seventy years of captivity he would bring his people back to their own land. Daniel added up the years since he had been deported to Babylon and realized that the captivity was almost over! Daniel began to pray. God's answer to Daniel's prayer was swift—and surprising! *Read Daniel 9.*

---

1. Daniel 9 has two parts. Verses 1-19 center around a prayer; verses 20-27 center around a message. Who speaks to whom in verses 1-19?

in verses 20-27?

---

2. God promised to release his people after seventy years of captivity. Then why did Daniel need to pray? (Jeremiah 29:10-14 may help.)

---

3. In verses 4-19, which aspects of God's character did Daniel appeal to as the basis of his requests?

---

4. Daniel also appealed to God on the basis of specific actions of grace and judgment God had performed for Israel. Which acts did he refer to, and why do you think he chose these?

---

5. What failures of the nation are cause for God's judgment?

6. Daniel consistently uses the plural pronoun *we* throughout the prayer. Why does Daniel include himself in the confession?

---

7. What specific insights about your own prayer life can you glean from Daniel's prayer?

---

8. In verse 24 Gabriel lists six things that will be accomplished for Israel and Jerusalem within seventy "sevens" (often interpreted as 490 years; see Leviticus 25:8-24). Which of these were accomplished when the people returned to Jerusalem from Babylon (after the first 49 years)?

Which were accomplished at the coming of the Anointed One (after 434 additional years)?

Are there any of the six that are not yet fully accomplished? Explain.

---

9. The 490-year clock begins with a "decree to restore and rebuild Jerusalem" (v. 25). This probably refers to a decree issued by the Persian king in 458 B.C. giving Ezra permission to reestablish Jerusalem as an officially recognized city (Ezra 7:3-26). Gabriel said that once the decree was issued, seven "sevens" and sixty-two "sevens" (483 years) would pass until the Anointed One would come and be "cut off" (vv. 25-26). This date corresponds with Jesus' thirtieth year (A.D. 26) when Jesus began his public ministry. What does this "date setting" tell you about how God's promises about the future will be fulfilled?

---

10. Verse 26 says that "the people of the ruler who will come will destroy the city and the sanctuary." The Romans destroyed Jerusalem and the temple in A.D. 70. How would you describe the course of events during the final period of seven years (vv. 26-27)?

---

11. Some Christians think the final "seven" was fulfilled in the time of Jerusalem's destruction by the Romans. Other Christians think the final seven years is still future and that this evil ruler will make his appearance on the world scene at that time. How do you react to the possibility of a wicked world ruler arising in our generation?

What does this chapter offer you (if anything) in the face of such a possibility?

Ask God to help you respond to his promises with assurance and expectant prayer.

Now or Later

Compose your own prayer of "national confession" based on Daniel's prayer in verses 4-19. Describe God's goodness and grace in the past and the nation's response or lack of it. Include a list of the sins that grieve God. Then pray the prayer to God. Be prepared to be challenged to be part of God's "solution" for one or more national problems.

11

A World
Out of Control

Daniel 10:1—11:35

Wars, terrorist acts, ethnic cleansing—our world moves from one crisis to another. What happens around us seems out of control. We find ourselves frustrated and frightened because we can't do anything to stop the terrible things that fill the headlines and flood our television screens.

GROUP DISCUSSION. What recent national or international crisis made you feel insecure or frightened? Explain why you felt that way.

PERSONAL REFLECTION. When you hear of bad things happening in other areas of the world or to other people, do you wonder why God doesn't intervene to stop what's happening?

What explanation do you give for God's apparent silence or inactivity?

In the last of Daniel's four visions recorded in chapters 7-12, Daniel gains new perspective on international events. He begins to see God's hand even in the clash of empires. *Read Daniel 10:1—11:1.*

---

1. If you had gone through this experience, what specific actions or words of the heavenly messenger would have encouraged or helped you? What would have concerned you?

2. How would Daniel's personal condition (10:2-3) and vision of the man (10:4-6) have caused him to react the way he did (10:7-11)?

3. What do the angel's words to Daniel tell you about God's response to those who seek him (10:12-14)?

4. How does Daniel's experience encourage you to be persistent in prayer?

5. The "prince of the Persian kingdom" (10:13) who resisted God's messenger probably refers to a powerful evil spirit who influenced the affairs of the Persian government. What does this "unveiling" of demonic activity in political affairs teach you about our world?

6. If an evil power could hinder an angel in Daniel's day, what does this indicate about your own need for help against Satan's forces?

7. *Read Daniel 11:2-35.* The conflict between Persia and Greece is described in 11:2-4. Based on your previous studies in Daniel, what names and events can you match with these predictions?

8. Daniel 11:5-35 is concerned with the conflict between two divisions of the Greek empire: the Syrian Seleucid family ("the king of the North") and the Egyptian Ptolemies ("the king of the South"). The focus is on a man we have met before—Antiochus Epiphanes. Daniel 11:21-24 describes his persecution of the people of Israel who had regathered in Palestine after the exile in Babylon. Summarize Antiochus's character and methods of operation from these verses.

9. Antiochus invaded Egypt the first time with relative success (11:25-28). The second time he met some opposition and in his frustration vented his anger on "the holy covenant," the Jewish religion (11:29-31). What do you learn from 11:32-35 about why God allows genuine believers to suffer under the hand of a godless tyrant?

10. All of chapter 11 was *future* to Daniel. However, 11:2-35 are *past* to us. Looking back, we can see how precisely God's plans came true. God really is in control! How can God's absolute authority and rule over history help you to stand firm when evil seems to triumph?

Pray for those in political authority over you. Ask God to rule and overrule in their decisions so that good and justice prevail.

Now or Later

Make a list of national, regional and local political leaders. Commit yourself to pray for them regularly. Write or e-mail at least one of the leaders to encourage him or her.

12

Darkness Before Deliverance

Daniel 11:36—12:13

We come to the end of our journey with mixed feelings. We are glad to be at our destination, but we will miss Daniel's presence. If you're like me, you're ending this study with a new appreciation for the majesty and authority of God, who can describe the future in detail, raise up kings and kingdoms and bring them to ruin, a God who can protect Daniel in the lions' den and who is as concerned about us.

GROUP DISCUSSION. What example or aspect of Daniel's character has helped you most to survive spiritually in a secular world?

PERSONAL REFLECTION. Realistically evaluate your own life and character. What strengths do you share with Daniel?

What weaknesses are exposed when you compare yourself to him?

The second part of Daniel's final vision projects Daniel into "the time of the end" of world history. The vision focuses on the nation of Israel but also gives us strong encouragement and hope during difficult times. *Read Daniel 11:36—12:13.*

---

1. Reading this passage during a time of persecution, what would sound like bad news to you? What would you read as good news?

2. Building from his portrait of Antiochus Epiphanes in 11:21-32, the heavenly messenger now focuses on the final oppressor of Israel who will arise at "the time of the end" (11:35-40). This "king" (following the example of Antiochus) will exalt himself as a god. How would you describe the "religious" character and actions of this king from 11:36-37?

3. This future king's god will be "a god of fortresses"—the ancient god of war and militarism (11:38-39). How do you see the influence of this god at work in our world today?

4. From 11:40-43 describe the military career of this future king.

5. "Reports from the east and the north" (11:44), which alarm the king, are apparently reports of other armies marching toward Israel for a final climactic battle. How would you describe the outcome of this battle from what you are told in this passage (11:44-45) and from what you have already learned about this future evil ruler (such as in 7:11, 25-27)?

6. The king's defeat and the deliverance of the godly come through the intervention of Michael, "the great prince" (12:1). How do you envision this intervention taking place?

7. How can this victory and the messenger's description of the resurrection (12:1-3) encourage us during times of tribulation?

8. Daniel was told to go on with his life even though he didn't fully understand all that he had been told. Describe a time when you had to trust God even though you didn't understand what he was doing in your life.

_____

9. Daniel's natural question after seeing this vision is "how long will it be before these astonishing things are fulfilled?" (12:6). How would you paraphrase the answer he received in 12:7?

_____

10. In 12:9-13 do you think the messenger avoided Daniel's last question (12:8), or did he answer it? Explain.

_____

11. In the course of your study in Daniel, what about the character of God strengthened you most spiritually?

How has this helped you worship and trust God more fully?

Ask God to help you cultivate a deeper trust in his ultimate authority and in his watchful care over you.

Now or Later

Looking at the world today, what groups of people would find Daniel's book most encouraging? Who might find Daniel's book terrifying?

Leader's Notes

MY GRACE IS SUFFICIENT FOR YOU. (2 COR 12:9)

Leading a Bible discussion can be an enjoyable and rewarding experience. But it can also be *scary*—especially if you've never done it before. If this is your feeling, you're in good company. When God asked Moses to lead the Israelites out of Egypt, he replied, "O Lord, please send someone else to do it"! (Ex 4:13). It was the same with Solomon, Jeremiah and Timothy, but God helped these people in spite of their weaknesses, and he will help you as well.

You don't need to be an expert on the Bible or a trained teacher to lead a Bible discussion. The idea behind these inductive studies is that the leader guides group members to discover for themselves what the Bible has to say. This method of learning will allow group members to remember much more of what is said than a lecture would.

These studies are designed to be led easily. As a matter of fact, the flow of questions through the passage from observation to interpretation to application is so natural that you may feel that the studies lead themselves. This study guide is also flexible. You can use it with a variety of groups—student, professional, neighborhood or church groups. Each study takes forty-five to sixty minutes in a group setting.

There are some important facts to know about group dynamics and encouraging discussion. The suggestions listed below should enable you to effectively and enjoyably fulfill your role as leader.

Preparing for the Study

1. Ask God to help you understand and apply the passage in your own life. Unless this happens, you will not be prepared to lead others. Pray too for the various members of the group. Ask God to open your hearts to the message of his Word and motivate you to action.

2. Read the introduction to the entire guide to get an overview of the entire book and the issues which will be explored.

3. As you begin each study, read and reread the assigned Bible passage to familiarize yourself with it.

4. This study guide is based on the New International Version of the Bible. It will help you and the group if you use this translation as the basis for your study and discussion.

5. Carefully work through each question in the study. Spend time in meditation and reflection as you consider how to respond.

6. Write your thoughts and responses in the space provided in the study guide. This will help you to express your understanding of the passage clearly.

7. It might help to have a Bible dictionary handy. Use it to look up any unfamiliar words, names or places. (For additional help on how to study a passage, see chapter five of *How to Lead a LifeBuilder Study* IVP, 2018.)

8. Consider how you can apply the Scripture to your life. Remember that the group will follow your lead in responding to the studies. They will not go any deeper than you do.

9. Once you have finished your own study of the passage, familiarize yourself with the leader's notes for the study you are leading. These are designed to help you in several ways. First, they tell you the purpose the study guide author had in mind when writing the study. Take time to think through how the study questions work together to accomplish that purpose. Second, the notes provide you with additional background information or suggestions on group dynamics for various questions. This information can be useful when people have difficulty understanding or answering a question. Third, the leader's notes can alert you to potential problems you may encounter during the study.

10. If you wish to remind yourself of anything mentioned in the leader's notes, make a note to yourself below that question in the study.

Leading the Study

1. Begin the study on time. Open with prayer, asking God to help the group to understand and apply the passage.

2. Be sure that everyone in your group has a study guide. Encourage the group to prepare beforehand for each discussion by reading the introduction to the guide and by working through the questions in the study.

3. At the beginning of your first time together, explain that these studies are meant to be discussions, not lectures. Encourage the members of the group to participate. However, do not put pressure on those who may be hesitant to speak during the first few sessions. You may want to suggest the following guidelines to your group.

☐ Stick to the topic being discussed.

☐ Your responses should be based on the verses which are the focus of the discussion and not on outside authorities such as commentaries or speakers.

☐ These studies focus on a particular passage of Scripture. Only rarely should you refer to other portions of the Bible. This allows for everyone to participate in in-depth study on equal ground.

☐ Anything said in the group is considered confidential and will not be discussed outside the group unless specific permission is given to do so.

☐ We will listen attentively to each other and provide time for each person present to talk.

☐ We will pray for each other.

4. Have a group member read the introduction at the beginning of the discussion.

5. Every session begins with a group discussion question. The question or activity is meant to be used before the passage is read. The question introduces the theme of the study and encourages group members to begin to open up. Encourage as many members as possible to participate, and be ready to get the discussion going with your own response.

This section is designed to reveal where our thoughts or feelings need to be transformed by Scripture. That is why it is especially important not to read the passage before the discussion question is asked. The passage will tend to color the honest reactions people would otherwise give because they are, of course, supposed to think the way the Bible does.

You may want to supplement the group discussion question with an ice-breaker to help people to get comfortable. See the community section of the *Small Group Starter Kit* (IVP, 1995) for more ideas.

You also might want to use the personal reflection question with your group. Either allow a time of silence for people to respond individually or discuss it together.

6. Have a group member (or members if the passage is long) read aloud the passage to be studied. Then give people several minutes to read the passage again silently so that they can take it all in.

7. Question 1 will generally be an overview question designed to briefly survey the passage. Encourage the group to look at the whole passage, but try to avoid getting sidetracked by questions or issues that will be addressed later in the study.

8. As you ask the questions, keep in mind that they are designed to be used just as they are written. You may simply read them aloud. Or you may prefer to express them in your own words.

There may be times when it is appropriate to deviate from the study guide. For example, a question may have already been answered. If so, move on to the next question. Or someone may raise an important question not covered in the guide. Take time to discuss it, but try to keep the group from going off on tangents.

9. Avoid answering your own questions. If necessary, repeat or rephrase them until they are clearly understood. Or point out something you read in the leader's notes to clarify the context or meaning. An eager group quickly becomes passive and silent if they think the leader will do most of the talking.

10. Don't be afraid of silence. People may need time to think about the question before formulating their answers.

11. Don't be content with just one answer. Ask, "What do the rest of you think?" or "Anything else?" until several people have given answers to the question.

12. Acknowledge all contributions. Try to be affirming whenever possible. Never reject an answer. If it is clearly off-base, ask, "Which verse led you to that conclusion?" or again, "What do the rest of you think?"

13. Don't expect every answer to be addressed to you, even though this will probably happen at first. As group members become more at ease, they will begin to truly interact with each other. This is one sign of healthy discussion.

14. Don't be afraid of controversy. It can be very stimulating. If you don't resolve an issue completely, don't be frustrated. Move on and keep it in mind for later. A subsequent study may solve the problem.

15. Periodically summarize what the group has said about the passage. This helps to draw together the various ideas mentioned and gives continuity to the study. But don't preach.

16. At the end of the Bible discussion you may want to allow group members a time of quiet to work on an idea under "Now or Later." Then discuss what you experienced. Or you may want to encourage group members to work on these ideas between meetings. Give an opportunity during the session for people to talk about what they are learning.

17. Conclude your time together with conversational prayer, adapting the prayer suggestion at the end of the study to your group. Ask for God's help in following through on the commitments you've made.

18. End on time.

Many more suggestions and helps are found in *How to Lead a LifeBuilder Study*.

Components of Small Groups

A healthy small group should do more than study the Bible. There are four components to consider as you structure your time together.

Nurture. Small groups help us to grow in our knowledge and love of God. Bible study is the key to making this happen and is the foundation of your small group.

Community. Small groups are a great place to develop deep friendships with other Christians. Allow time for informal interaction before and after each study. Plan activities and games that will help you get to know each other. Spend time having fun together—going on a picnic or cooking dinner together.

Worship and prayer. Your study will be enhanced by spending time praising God together in prayer or song. Pray for each other's needs—and keep track of how God is answering prayer in your group. Ask God to help you to apply what you are learning in your study.

Outreach. Reaching out to others can be a practical way of applying what you are learning, and it will keep your group from becoming self-focused. Host a series of evangelistic discussions for your friends or neighbors. Clean up the yard of an elderly friend. Serve at a soup kitchen together, or spend a day working in the community.

Many more suggestions and helps in each of these areas are found in the *Small Group Starter Kit.* You will also find information on building a small group. Reading through the starter kit will be worth your time.

General Suggestions for Studies 1-7 (Daniel 1—6).

Daniel's life and character provide help to those of us who are trying to live a distinctively Christian life in the context of a secular society. The theme of godly living in an ungodly world is the focus in each of these studies. The application questions particularly have been formulated with that central concept in mind. Therefore, as you lead a group it is important to apply the spiritual principles in as many ways as possible to the individual cultural context of your group—a university campus, an office complex, the business or professional world, your neighborhood. How does Daniel's example change my life? should be the underlying question in each group session.

These narrative chapters are not difficult to understand. Their value in spiritual growth will become evident as the truths they teach are lived out. Strive to keep the study from becoming simply an academic analysis of ancient events. Instead, push for both clear understanding of what God's Word says and how it should affect the people in your study group.

As mentioned in the introduction, some scholars have denied the authenticity and prophetic nature of the book of Daniel. The group leader ought to have at least a basic understanding of the arguments raised against Daniel and how other scholars have defended the historicity of the book. Helpful resources are: Josh McDowell, *Daniel in the Critics' Den* (San Bernardino, Calif.: Campus Crusade for Christ, 1979); and Roland K. Harrison, *Introduction to the Old Testament* (Grand Rapids, Mich.: Eerdmans, 1969), pp. 1105-34. You may also want to read a good commentary on Daniel as a supplement to your study. I have found these helpful: Joyce Baldwin, *Daniel* (Downers Grove, Ill.: InterVarsity Press, 1978); Leon Wood, *A Commentary on Daniel* (Grand Rapids, Mich.: Zondervan, 1973); and Ajith Fernando, *Daniel*, NIV Application Commentary (Grand Rapids, Mich.: Zondervan, 1998).

Study 1. Daniel 1. Have You Got What It Takes?

Purpose: To be challenged with the importance of taking a stand for biblical truth and personal conviction.

General note. You should be familiar with the introduction to the study guide. It might be profitable to give a brief summary of the historical context of Daniel, perhaps by using a time line to visualize the main events and to show where Daniel fits in the flow of Old Testament history.

Question 2. Daniel's Hebrew name meant "God is my Judge." His new Babylonian name, *Belteshazzar,* meant "may Bel protect the king." (Bel was the chief Babylonian deity.) The word translated "youths" in verse 4 is normally used to refer to a young teenager, twelve to fourteen years old. Daniel must have been quite young, since seventy-three years later he was still alive and active (Dan 10:1).

Question 4. The king's food produced two problems for Daniel and his friends. First, it was the custom of the king to offer his food to idols before it was eaten. Daniel viewed eating that food as the first step toward spiritual compromise. Second, the diet would have included foods that God had declared unclean for his people. Pork was a delicacy in Babylon. Horsemeat was commonly eaten. Both were prohibited (see Lev 11:2-8). So rather than offend God, Daniel made up his mind not to become defiled.

Question 5. Daniel only objected to his new culture when that culture came into direct conflict with the clear instruction of God's Word. Christians today can measure an activity they want to pursue against the teaching of the Bible. If the Bible speaks against that activity, God's will is clear. If the Bible allows an activity or is silent on the issue, the Christian then must take other factors into consideration. Will this activity cause another Christian to stumble into sin because of my example? Will this activity enhance my ability to share the message of Christ with those around me? Would I be comfortable inviting Jesus to accompany me?

Question 6. Daniel did not organize a protest march against the Babylonian program. Instead he approached his superior with a wise alternate plan and was willing to bear the responsibility for its outcome.

Question 8. Verses 9 and 17 give God the ultimate credit for the success of Daniel and his friends, but they were involved in the process too. They worked hard and kept their lives pure. They also focused their energy on doing well to bring glory to God.

For the next study. Point out the "Group Discussion" question in study two. They will want to give it some thought beforehand.

Study 2. Daniel 2:1-30. A Disturbing Dream.
Purpose: To demonstrate God's faithfulness to us in a time of personal crisis.

Question 2. The four groups of men summoned by Nebuchadnezzar in Daniel 2:2 made up the king's "cabinet." They were his advisers in matters of state. They were also closely connected with the Babylonian religious system and claimed to have the ability to predict the future. All these men were deeply involved in the occult. It is significant that Daniel makes a clear distinction between the methods of the occultic priests and his reliance on truth revealed to him by the true God (see 2:27-28).

Verse 1 says that this happened in the second year of Nebuchadnezzar's reign. He became the king just after his conquest of Jerusalem in 605 B.C., when Daniel was taken captive. Therefore, this was also the second year of Daniel's training.

Question 4. Be sure to point out how Daniel's "wisdom and tact" (v. 14) are demonstrated in this crisis. Daniel resisted his natural inclination to panic and wisely gave God time to work. He also was willing to bear the consequences of his plan's failure. Daniel refused to blame others for the crisis and courageously stepped forward to meet the challenge.

Question 7. Daniel's boldness didn't rest on his own cleverness or ability but on a confident trust that God wouldn't fail him. Usually our first reaction in a crisis is to use our own resources and power to solve the problem. We seem to turn to God only when every other avenue has been exhausted.

Question 8. Daniel prefaced his interpretation of the dream with a lesson on the nature of the true God. The gods in Nebuchadnezzar's experience were limited in their power. Daniel's God was the God of all power and knowledge. Nebuchadnezzar thought Israel's military defeat was a sign that Babylon's gods were more powerful than Israel's God, but he was mistaken. The God of Israel was the one who *allowed* Babylon to conquer Israel (Dan 1:1-2).

Study 3. Daniel 2:31-49. Facing the Future.
Purpose: To explore God's future program as it was revealed to Daniel and to gain a new appreciation for God's control of history.

General note. The main concern you may face in this study is the clash between various schools of thought on end-times events. The key interpretive disagreement centers on where our present age "fits" in the flow of earthly kingdoms represented in the statue. Focus the group's attention on the particular prophetic passage covered in the study and try not to let the discussion go on a tangent about entire systems of prophetic interpretation.

Question 3. God had placed his people under the rule of a powerful king. Just a few years before, the prophet Jeremiah announced that God had granted Nebuchadnezzar authority over all the nations of that region and even over the animals within his realm (see Jer 27:6-7, 14). While Daniel's declaration that Nebuchadnezzar was the head of gold would have fueled the king's pride, he must also have been shaken to hear that his kingdom would come to an end (v. 39).

Question 4. Daniel makes it clear that the kingdoms following Babylon will be "inferior" (v. 39) in quality. Moving down the statue, the metals decrease in value, but increase in relative strength.

Question 5. This identification seems most likely since Media and Persia are viewed later in the book as one kingdom not two (8:20). The kingdom following Medo-Persia is identified as Greece in 8:21. Some interpreters, however, have identified the kingdoms as Media (silver), Persia (bronze) and Greece (iron). Each successive kingdom was larger in territory and lasted longer than the Babylonian kingdom, but each was inferior in organization and overall treatment of the people of Israel. Each succeeding kingdom relied more and more on military oppression to control the people under their domination.

Question 6. The immense figure stands on fragile feet of pottery mixed with iron. Many Bible scholars believe that these "ten toes of clay and iron" represent the weakness of the late Roman empire. Others believe that the ten toes represent a still future coalition of nations that will exist at Jesus' second coming.

Question 7. God's kingdom suddenly emerges and removes all human governments and institutions. Humanity's control will not gradually evolve into the day of the Lord but will be suddenly and permanently replaced by the supernatural inauguration of God's kingdom.

Question 8. Christians have taken both sides of this question. Try to focus the group's attention on just this passage. If all we knew about God's kingdom was what we find in Daniel 2, how would you answer the question? Don't get bogged down in lengthy debate. Daniel doesn't give us the complete answer.

Question 9. Nebuchadnezzar acknowledges the superior power of Daniel's God but does not come to personal trust in the true God until later in his life (Dan 4).

Study 4. Daniel 3. Bow or Burn!

Purpose: To understand the risks and rewards of obedience to God and his Word.

Question 2. While it isn't possible to prove a connection between the statue in Nebuchadnezzar's dream in chapter 2 and the image in chapter 3, such a connection seems likely. In chapter 2 Nebuchadnezzar was only the head of gold. Other kingdoms would eventually replace his, and God's kingdom would ultimately be supreme. Perhaps this thought irritated Nebuchadnezzar who probably wanted to think his own kingdom would last forever. In response (perhaps), he builds an image in chapter 3, that is gold from head to foot. Is this a challenge to what God had declared? Let the group decide!

The dimensions of this image may raise some questions. The text says that the image was "ninety feet high and nine feet wide." Those dimensions would produce a grotesque figure. It would be comparable to a person who was six feet tall and seven inches wide! The image probably stood on a base and the total height (base and statue) was ninety feet. Archaeologists have discovered a brick pedestal in Totul Dura ("mounds of Dura") just six miles south of the site of ancient Babylon. The pedestal ruin is forty-five feet square and twenty feet high. The French archaeologist who discovered it, Julius Oppert, believed that it was the base of the image described in Daniel 3.

Question 3. Another question raised in connection with this account is, Where was Daniel? Certainly Daniel would not have bowed to Nebuchadnezzar's image either. Why wasn't he thrown into the fire with his three friends? We aren't told in the passage so we don't know for sure where Daniel was. Daniel, however, held a high rank in the government (see Dan 2:48) and could have been absent on official business.

Question 4. Nebuchadnezzar was willing to give these men another chance to obey his order. You might want to ask the group to come up with a list of rationalizations that Shadrach, Meshach and Abednego could have used if they had chosen to disobey God.

Question 6. The three men realized that God had the power to change their circumstances, but also that God may choose not to act. Regardless, they obeyed and were willing to bear the consequences of their decision. They would rather suffer loss (even of their lives) than disobey God.

Question 7. The purpose of this question is not to get the group sidetracked into a discussion about healing or the purpose of suffering. The point you need to focus on is that while God is able to end our suffering, he may not choose to do so. But even then we are challenged to trust him and continue to live obediently before him.

Question 10. The best time to prepare for a challenge to your faith is not when the challenge comes but long before. These men (like Daniel in 1:8) had already decided that they would obey God's Word regardless of the pressure they faced. Their decision was made long before the challenge came. Encourage your group to make a commitment to obedience now to prepare them for decisions under pressure they will face in the future.

Study 5. Daniel 4. Our God Reigns!

Purpose: To show that God is in control of his world and that he humbles those who are proud.

Question 1. Nebuchadnezzar wrote 4:1-3 after his experience of humiliation described later in the chapter. Most likely Nebuchadnezzar came to believe in the true God through his experience. In chapter 3 Nebuchadnezzar praised the God of Shadrach, Meshach and Abednego; in chapter 4 he praises the same God but now in terms of personal faith.

Question 3. The aspect of God's character explained and illustrated in Daniel 4 is usually referred to as "God's sovereignty." God is sovereign over his creation. He has absolute authority and control over human history. God is free to do whatever he desires to accomplish his will. Nothing happens in our world or in our lives that God does not cause or permit to happen. God's sovereign authority does not eliminate human choice. God works all things together to bring good to his children and ultimate glory to himself.

Other passages on God's absolute authority include Genesis 45:7-8, 50:19-20; Deuteronomy 32:39; 1 Chronicles 29:12; 2 Chronicles 20:6; Isaiah 45:6-22, 46:9-11; Romans 9:14-18, 13:1; Ephesians 1:3-12.

Question 4. This question will probably generate considerable discussion. Evil rulers may at times rise to power and pursue policies of incredible oppression and injustice. God is not powerless in those situations. He is not the source of evil but permits evil to run its course in order to accomplish his ultimate purposes. Point out that God will judge unrepentant leaders for their sin. Divine authority does not erase human responsibility. Nebuchadnezzar is an excellent example of that truth!

Question 6. Even after judgment was pronounced God extended grace to Nebuchadnezzar. God gave the king a full year to repent and turn humbly to God for forgiveness, but Nebuchadnezzar refused. Later in Daniel, God will immediately carry out his judgment on another proud king (Dan 5:24-26, 30).

Question 7. The medical term for Nebuchadnezzar's condition is boanthropy—a rare condition in which a person behaves like a bull or cow. An eyewitness observation of this condition can be found in Roland Harrison, *Introduction to the Old Testament* (Grand Rapids, Mich.: Eerdmans, 1969), pp. 1116-17.

Question 8. Nebuchadnezzar's praise to God and affirmation of trust certainly don't sound forced. He seems to joyfully embrace God's actions as just and right—even the actions that brought him personal pain.

Question 10. Our God is not a frivolous God. He always has a purpose for what he does and what he allows. God has a purpose for every believer too! His goal is to conform us to the likeness of Jesus Christ. Everything God allows in our lives, even the experiences that bring pain, will move us closer to that goal.

Study 6. Daniel 5. The Handwriting on the Wall.
Purpose: To explore the role a committed Christian can play in influencing a decaying society.
Question 2. Shortly after Nebuchadnezzar's return to sanity (described in the last verses of chapter 4), he died. The date was 562 B.C. The events in chapter 5 took place in 539 B.C., twenty-three years later.

In 556 B.C., a king named Nabonidus took the throne and reigned the last twenty-five years of the empire's existence. He was the king when the city fell to the Persians. Critical scholars have been quick to point to Daniel's "error" in verse 1 where he writes of King Belshazzar. For over two thousand years no record of Belshazzar was found. In the early 1900s, however, archaeologists began to dig up the ruins of ancient Babylon. Amazingly the name *Bel-sharutsur* (Belshazzar) began to appear. Finally a British archaeologist published an inscription from Babylon that said Belshazzar was the son of Nabonidus. Furthermore, because Nabonidus liked to travel so much, he entrusted the kingship to Belshazzar in 553 B.C. Belshazzar was the coregent with Nabonidus for fourteen years. That also explains why Belshazzar offered to make Daniel "third highest ruler in the kingdom" (v. 7). Instead of being a mistake, the reference to Belshazzar demonstrates the accuracy of Daniel's book.

Belshazzar's confidence rested on the fortifications of the city of Babylon. The walled part of the city was sixty miles in circumference. The wall itself was 150 feet high and 87 feet thick. Four chariots could ride abreast on top of the wall. Around the wall was a thirty-foot moat. The city was considered impregnable.

This source of Babylonian smugness became their downfall. Fresh water was supplied to Babylon by a canal from the Euphrates River that flowed through the city. According to the ancient Greek historian Herodotus, the Persian army dug another canal to divert the water. On the night of Belshazzar's feast, they opened the new canal and marched into Babylon on the riverbed. There was almost no struggle. While the Babylonian soldiers slept and Belshazzar feasted, the Medes and the Persians conquered the impenetrable city.
Question 3. The words written on the wall were normal Aramaic words. (Aramaic was the language of Babylon.) The wise men, however, could not

even read the words much less explain their significance or meaning (5:8, 17). Daniel could read the words ("measured, measured, weighed, divided in two") and only Daniel had access to God's "commentary" on what the words meant for Belshazzar and the Babylonians.

Question 4. Belshazzar knew about Nebuchadnezzar's experience (v. 22) but refused to learn from it.

Question 7. Knowing what the Bible teaches and understanding Daniel's experiences with God will not make much difference in our lives unless we apply the truth to how we live. Nebuchadnezzar and Belshazzar reflected the same arrogance that can rise up in our hearts and be displayed in our attitudes. God will deal as harshly with pride today as he did in Daniel's day!

Question 8. Contrast God's immediate judgment on Belshazzar with God's delayed judgment on Nebuchadnezzar (4:27-31). Was it because Belshazzar had full knowledge of Nebuchadnezzar's experience but refused to humble himself before God that he was judged so quickly?

Study 7. Daniel 6. On the Menu at the Lions' Club.

Purpose: To encourage Christians to persevere in their commitments to the Lord in spite of opposition or oppression.

Question 1. Each of the groups in this chapter were related to Daniel through his official position in the Persian govvernment. Daniel had authority over the satraps (local provincial governors). The administrators were Daniel's coworkers and Darius was Daniel's boss.

The critical question in chapter 6 is the identity of Darius the Mede. He was apparently the man to whom Cyrus, the Persian monarch, entrusted the area around Babylon. Daniel refers to Darius as "the king." Darius reorganized the government under Persian authority. Because of his wisdom Daniel was included in the top leadership of the new government.

Question 2. Daniel wasn't doing anything wrong ("corrupt") nor was he failing to do what was right and honorable ("negligent"). These men knew that they could only bring Daniel down if they set a trap that would force him to obey God rather than the king.

Question 4. Daniel's enemies obviously lied to Darius by implying that all the administrators had agreed to this decree. Daniel certainly hadn't agreed but once a royal decree had been issued under Persian law, it couldn't be rescinded or changed. (Compare a similar situation in the story of Esther, Esther 1:19; 8:8.) Darius was flattered by the proposal and foolishly signed the decree. In the pagan cultures of the ancient world the king or ruler was often portrayed as a god. It would not be unusual, then, to offer prayer to the king.

Question 5. Hundreds of years before this event King Solomon warned the people of Israel that a day might come when they would find themselves in a land of captivity. Then the people were to "pray to [God] toward the land, . . . toward the city [God had] chosen" (see 1 Kings 8:46-51).

Question 6. Darius made every effort to reverse the judgment on Daniel. He obviously valued Daniel's friendship and leadership. Daniel obviously had talked to Darius about God, because Darius realized that Daniel's God had the power to rescue him (6:16, 20).

Under the Medes and Persians criminals were thrown into a cave or pit filled with half-starved lions. Under the Babylonians, criminals were executed in a furnace of fire (Dan 3:6). The Medes and Persians worshiped a fire-god and so refused to execute criminals in the same way they offered sacrifices to their god.

Question 7. Rulers (ancient and modern) can be exceptionally cruel in their revenge. Here not only the men involved in the plot against Daniel but their wives and children were executed. Remind your group that this was Darius's decision not Daniel's. It was the custom of ancient kings to eliminate the entire family of anyone perceived as an enemy.

General Suggestions for Studies 8-12 (Daniel 7—12). The second part of the book of Daniel focuses on Daniel's prophetic visions. As explained in the introduction, the interpretation of these prophecies has been the source of much debate. Try not to allow the group session to become a debate over which system of interpretation is correct. The questions center on the text itself, and that is where the discussion should focus. You also need to be wary of your own presuppositions. Don't be guilty of promoting your own pet view either! The purpose of the group discussion is to understand Daniel's message and to apply it to our lives. While these chapters are more difficult than the first six, they are no less powerful for those who seek to understand them.

Study 8. Daniel 7. A Prophetic Panorama.
Purpose: To instill confidence in God's plan for history and in his power to do what he promises.

General note. The visions recorded in chapters 7-12 were given at various times in Daniel's life. When Daniel's writings were collected, the historical and biographical material were included first, then the prophetic material. Each was grouped together because of similarity in content. This vision fits historically between chapters 4 and chapter 5 (approx. 553 B.C.).

Question 2. The experience Daniel had is called both a dream (v. 1) and a "vision" (v. 2). Normally dreams come when we sleep and visions when awake. God spoke to Daniel throughout the night as Daniel passed in and out of sleep. The essential point to remember is that all these messages and images came from God. God used a variety of techniques to speak to Old Testament prophets (Heb 1:1-4).

As the members of the group share what questions they would have asked the interpreter of the vision (v. 16), don't try to answer those questions at this point. The exercise is to get the group to see that God didn't explain every detail or even the details we think are important. God focuses instead on the essential features of the vision from the perspective of his ultimate plan.

Question 3. For passages in which the sea is a symbol for the nations of the world, see Isaiah 17:12-13; 57:20 and Luke 21:25. God often uses symbolism to communicate his message. Nebuchadnezzar's vision of the "tree" in Daniel 4 is another example. In this chapter, four kingdoms arise from the swirling turmoil of the nations.

Question 4. As in all biblical parables and visions not every minute detail is described. The important features of each beast are listed, and they parallel certain qualities of the kingdom each represents. Don't get bogged down in minor disagreements of interpretation.

The four beasts probably correspond to the four parts of the statue in Daniel 2. The lion is the same as the head of gold (Babylon). The bear is the chest and arms of silver (Medo-Persia). The leopard is the belly and thighs of bronze (Greece). The fourth beast is the legs of iron (Rome).

Question 7. Jesus identified himself as this "son of man" in Mark 14:62. He is clearly distinct from the Ancient of Days (God the Father) and yet displays the same absolute power. The term "son of man" also links this heavenly deliverer with the human inhabitants of the world he comes to rescue and rule.

Question 8. The saints will not conquer the kingdoms of the world; they will receive a kingdom from the one who will conquer (Rev 19:11-16).

Question 9. The ten horns in this vision parallel the ten toes of the image in Daniel 2. Both ten-nation confederations emerge in some way from the fierce fourth kingdom. The "other horn" in Daniel 7 is a new element not revealed in Daniel 2. This "king" (v. 24) will subdue the other kings or kingdoms and will speak in opposition to God. Some Christians believe this was a Roman emperor like Nero who persecuted the early church. Other Christians believe the "other horn" refers to a still future ruler who will rise in opposition to God and his people (compare Rev 13:1-8).

Question 11. God is emphasizing the fact that this powerful ruler will be brought to judgment at the initiative of God, not a human tribunal. The "trial" picture also conveys the full accountability and precise justice that will be carried out against this evil king.

Study 9. Daniel 8. Superpowers in Conflict.

Purpose: To demonstrate how accurately God predicts the future and how events take place precisely as he declares they will.

Question 1. It might be helpful to have a dry-erase board or posterboard set up to list each image in one column and what it represents in another.

Question 2. The coalition of the Medes and the Persians was the instrument God used to conquer the Babylonian empire. The two horns of the ram (in Daniel's vision) are unequal in size because the Persians were more numerous than the Medes. Eventually this empire was simply called the Persian empire.

Questions 3-4. As the Persians expanded their empire westward they began to drive Greek-speaking people out of Asia Minor (modern-day Turkey) and eventually came into direct conflict with the Greek city-states. The Persian armies failed to conquer the Greek peninsula. Alexander the Great brought Greek revenge on the Persians when he conquered and dismantled their vast empire in a few short years. Some historical facts about the rivalry between the Greeks and the Persians will add depth to the symbolic descriptions given in these verses. A good commentary on Daniel will provide the needed background. You should remind the group that God was giving this detailed information to Daniel two hundred years before the events took place.

Question 5. Antiochus Epiphanes (an-tie'-o-cuss ee-pi'-fan-eez) is a key figure in this chapter and in chapter 11. This may be a good place to briefly sketch the career of this man for the group. A commentary on Daniel, a Bible dictionary or a historical survey of the intertestamental period in Israel will give you some help. See, for example, F. F. Bruce, *Israel & the Nations* (Downers Grove, Ill.: InterVarsity Press, 1998), pp. 134-53.

You can read the account of the oppression of the Jews by Antiochus and the resulting Maccabean revolt in 1 Maccabees (especially chapters 1-4). First Maccabees is a book in the Apocrypha. You can find it in a Bible that includes the Apocrypha, or as a separate volume. The Roman Catholic Church views the Apocrypha as Scripture. Most Protestants and Jews do not accept it as part of the Bible.

Question 6. Twice (vv. 19, 26) Gabriel makes it clear that this vision concerns the "time of the end" or "the distant future." Many Bible students believe that Antiochus Epiphanes is a picture of the final evil ruler who will appear on the world scene just before the establishment of Christ's kingdom. This question can easily lead to speculation and debate about a future "Antichrist." Try to keep the group focused on Daniel's vision and the character of this evil ruler.

Question 8. God's authority (or sovereignty) is a theme in every chapter of Daniel. Daniel and his people were oppressed, conquered and made captives of a pagan nation, but God had not forgotten them. God was at work even in the worst circumstances to accomplish his own good and wise purposes.

Question 9. This chapter brings us back to the problem of evil. How can a good God allow such bad things to happen to his own people? God wants us to see that his plan for human history includes allowing evil to run its course. Just because wicked rulers gain strength for a while, we should not think that God is absent or unconcerned.

Now or Later. The New Testament makes predictions about our future as Christians. For example, Jesus promised that he would return to earth (Jn 14:2-3)—a prophecy emphasized repeatedly in the New Testament (Acts 1:11; 1 Thess 4:13-18; Rev 19:11-16). The Bible also says that we will stand before Christ to give an account of how we have used our abilities and resources (Rom 14:10-11; 2 Cor 5:10). If Daniel's predictions were so precisely fulfilled, can we expect less of the Bible's predictions that are yet to be fulfilled?

Study 10. Daniel 9. Kneeling on God's Promises.

Purpose: To encourage expectant prayer because of God's promises.

Question 2. The people's prayers would indicate to the Lord that the seventy years of separation from their homeland had accomplished what God desired. The people had returned to the Lord with wholehearted obedience and loyalty.

Question 6. Daniel is one of only three major Bible characters about whom no sin or personal failure is recorded. (Jesus and Abraham's grandson Joseph are the other two.) Daniel certainly did sin at times but his life as a whole reflected consistent integrity and joyful obedience to God. Daniel includes himself in the prayer of confession as a way of identifying himself with his people. Daniel probably had not lived among the exiles from Judah during his seventy years in Babylon, but he must have sensed the same despair as the people because of their separation from the land God had given to them.

Question 8. This prophecy of "Daniel's seventy weeks" or "seventy sevens" is probably the most widely debated prophecy in the book. There are several different interpretations, especially for the timing of the final period of seven years. Try not to debate questions that have no certain answers. Focus on what the text actually says and base your conclusions on what is clearly revealed.

Question 9. Actually, students of Daniel's book have proposed four decrees about Jerusalem as possible starting dates for Daniel's 490 years: (1) Cyrus's decree to rebuild the temple in 539 B.C. (Ezra 1:1-4), (2) Darius's decree in 519 B.C. (Ezra 6:1-12), (3) Artaxerxes' decree to Ezra in 458 B.C., and (4)

Artaxerxes' decree to Nehemiah in 444 B.C. (Neh 2:1-10). In my opinion, the third decree best fits the framework of the prophecy.

Some may question the date of Jesus' baptism (A.D. 26). It is likely that Jesus was born between 6 and 4 B.C., so his thirtieth year would fall at about A.D. 26 (Lk 3:23).

Question 10. The group may feel frustrated or confused because they can't fully solve the riddle of the prophecy. They should realize, however, that Christians have wrestled with the meaning of these verses for centuries. The main point is that just as God was in control of Israel's seventy-year captivity, so he will be in control of Israel's future and his restoration of all things through the Messiah. These were strong words of hope to Daniel—and to us!

Study 11. Daniel 10:1—11:35. A World Out of Control.

Purpose: To assure believers that in spite of the opposition of human beings and even demonic beings, God's plan for his people will be fulfilled.

Question 3. The messenger was sent by God three weeks earlier—at the beginning of Daniel's fast. The messenger was hindered from coming to Daniel by the opposition of a powerful evil angel.

Question 5. The purpose of this question is not to lead the group into envisioning weird scenarios of demonic attack on a nation's capital but to point out the very real influence exerted by Satan on national leaders. Some in your group may find it hard to accept the idea that demon forces are at work today in the same way they were in Daniel's day. Some New Testament references to Satan's activity in the world (1 Jn 4:1-3; 5:19; Eph 2:2) and against Christians (Eph 6:11-12; 1 Pet 5:8-9; Jas 4:7) may help to answer that objection.

Question 7. The fourth Persian king was Xerxes (ruled 486-465 B.C.), who mounted a great campaign to conquer the Greek peninsula. The "mighty king" (v. 3) was Alexander the Great (ruled 336-323 B.C.), who retaliated against Persia and seized the Persian empire for Greece. Alexander died at the age of thirty-two and his vast empire was divided not among his sons but among his four generals.

Question 9. The "ships of the western coastlands" is a reference to the Romans. Roman armies under Popilius Laenas met Antiochus's army in Egypt and forced him to retreat back to Syria. On the way back home Antiochus attacked and ravaged Judea and Jerusalem.

Study 12. Daniel 11:36—12:13. Darkness Before Deliverance.

Purpose: To find comfort in the future history of Israel as it faced great oppression and then final deliverance from God.

Question 2. All attempts to fit the details of 11:40-45 into the known career of Antiochus Epiphanes have been futile. Those who try to make this identification simply assume that these prophecies were never fulfilled—a conclusion totally out of character with the rest of the book. It is much better to see these verses as describing a future king who will arise at "the time of the end" (11:35). Antiochus was a prototype of the final evil oppressor of Israel.

Question 4. Some commentators identify the king of the north as the future evil king. In my opinion, 11:40 indicates that the king of the north and the king of the south both engage the evil king in battle. The evil king (apparently) will defeat them both.

Question 5. While the future king seems invincible for a time, he will ultimately meet his end and be defeated by the return of God's eternal king, Jesus, who will set up an eternal kingdom.

Question 6. God's angels are involved in the final battle against human wickedness and oppression. Revelation 12 pictures a war in heaven between Michael, surrounded by the angels of God, and Satan, surrounded by his angels. In the end Satan (and his earthly instrument, the evil king) are destroyed.

Question 7. This is the only use of the phrase "everlasting life" in the Old Testament. Before the resurrection of Jesus not much was revealed about life after death. Old Testament hints of the resurrection of the body can be found in Job 14:11-14; 19:25-27; Psalms 16:10; 49:15; Isaiah 25:8; 26:19; Hosea 13:14.

Question 8. The phrase "a time, times and half a time" was used in Daniel 7:25 to describe the duration of oppression of the saints by the "little horn"— another figure of the future oppressor of Israel. Some scholars have linked the phrase with the three and a half years of Revelation (compare Revelation 11:2— "42 months"; Revelation 11:3—"1,260 days"; Revelation 12:14). From the time of the evil king's ascendancy over God's people, three and a half measures of time will pass until God's people are humbled ("the power of the holy people has been finally broken") and the king is removed by divine intervention.

Question 9. The messenger does not answer Daniel's question directly but gives further calculations that apply to the end of human history.

Question 10. This question is designed to bring the focus of the study back to the absolute authority and goodness of God. Encourage the members of the group to express what the study of Daniel has meant in their personal growth and spiritual development.

Douglas Connelly is the senior pastor at Davison Missionary Church, near Flint, Michigan. He is also the author of Angels Around Us *(InterVarsity Press) and* The Bible for Blockheads *(Zondervan) as well as seventeen LifeBuilder Bible Studies.*